10/8/21   1.- 00

The Web of Words
Teacher's Book

The Web of Words

Exploring literature
through language

Teacher's Book

*Ronald Carter and
Michael N. Long*

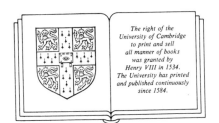

The right of the
University of Cambridge
to print and sell
all manner of books
was granted by
Henry VIII in 1534.
The University has printed
and published continuously
since 1584.

Cambridge University Press
Cambridge
New York   New Rochelle
Melbourne   Sydney

Published by the Press Syndicate of the University of Cambridge
The Pitt Building, Trumpington Street, Cambridge CB2 1RP
32 East 57th Street, New York, NY 10022, USA
10 Stamford Road, Oakleigh, Melbourne 3166, Australia

© Cambridge University Press 1987

First published 1987

Printed in Great Britain at the Bath Press, Avon

ISBN 0 521 33926 X Teacher's Book
ISBN 0 521 27772 8 Student's Book
ISBN 0 521 30778 3 Cassette

WD

Contents

Section I Introduction

Background to English language and literature teaching

In recent years there has often been an uneasy relationship between the teaching of English language and the teaching of English literature, especially in the non-native speaker context.

All too often literature has been omitted entirely from the course, and this has been explained away by lack of time or at worst branded as an irrelevance. In some courses literature has been studied at the same time as language but segregated from it, as though there were little common ground between the two. On such courses the literature component has often been of the survey type; numerous facts about periods and writers, as well as lists of titles of famous works being given. Elsewhere literature has been studied as a sort of 'special purpose English', as a source of 'facts' about life, philosophy or morals. *The Web of Words* differs from these approaches in that it treats the study of English language and literature as an integrated process.

Aims

The main aim of this book is to help the learner to understand and appreciate literary texts. It focuses on certain features of language in order to generate an appreciation of the style, effects and techniques of writing. Thus, while helping learners to read and appreciate authentic literary sources, the book elicits a response to language. The exercises develop language competence and literary appreciation in relation to each other. With its integrated approach, the book also aims to stimulate language learning and generate a real interest in literature – not least a desire to read more of texts of which only extracts are used.

Variety

The Web of Words presents the learner with a wide range of texts, and at the same time uses a variety of techniques and exercises in exploiting those texts. This variety increases learner motivation and provides greater flexibility: each text can be studied by means of the 'approach' best suited to it. The 'approaches' do not, of course, claim to deliver literary competence. They lay a basis of preliminary techniques and procedures which are designed to give students increasing confidence in their own understanding and appreciation.

Grading and organisation

The Web of Words provides an integrated 'programme' of language and literature. It is not a series of graded language exercises and activities. It is not possible, in dealing with literary texts, to follow the progressive sequencing or neat unit length of a good language course book. Here the progression is based on our assessment of the difficulty or sophistication of analytical tasks. It is therefore not absolutely necessary to work through the book from beginning to end, in the manner of a conventional course book. The final unit does, however, combine several of the approaches used in other units. The unit promotes various kinds of discussion based on play extracts, poems and a complete short story, thus extending and consolidating the work done in earlier units.

The book provides the teacher with flexibility in designing a course. He or she may choose to work through the book unit by unit, or select a single text from each unit in a series of lessons, thereby varying the 'approaches'. It would also be possible to apply several 'approaches' to the same text. (While this may have some advantages, it should be treated with caution since it runs the risk of 'doing a text to death'.)

'Approaches'

Each unit develops a possible classroom 'approach' to the study of text. The classroom work is designed to equip learners with a range of reading strategies for interpreting and appreciating literary text. Learners must, of course, realise that not all 'approaches' work equally well for every text and that no single 'approach' can be advocated as more successful than all others. To achieve this perception, 'approaches' are sometimes re-cycled in subsequent units, and sometimes a text is re-cycled but used with a different 'approach'. It is most important for learners to recognise the usefulness of different 'approaches' and learn both how to apply and how to combine them.

Techniques

Each 'approach' incorporates features of well-tried and widely practised techniques from language teaching and elementary linguistics. These are frequently developed with activities which use pair or group work. The overall 'approach' of *The Web of Words* seeks to minimise the time spent by the teacher controlling the lesson and transmitting information about the text, author, period or genre. Learners are guided towards making their own judgements about a text.

Awareness of language features

Any learner who has sufficient English to study the literary texts in this book must have an adequate knowledge of grammar, vocabulary and phonology, although these may not have been taught systematically or explicitly in the learner's acquisition of English. A greater awareness of how these language features work will provide important clues to under- standing the nuances of a writer's use of language. As well as the more obvious areas of grammar and vocabulary, discourse and cohesion are considered in Units 6 and 7, while in Unit 8 several levels of language are explored simultaneously. The exercises are not, however, designed to produce exhaustive stylistic analyses. This is neither within the scope of this book nor the anticipated level of the student. Though it is stressed that language-based activities are continuously relevant, the teacher must never let the learners lose sight of the fact that they are dealing with an art form. This art form orders and patterns actions, ideas, characters and belief-systems; indeed, anything that can be referred to by language, as well as the language itself.

Level

The Web of Words is appropriate for upper-intermediate and advanced learners of English. Though no particular age range is envisaged, the selection of texts would be widely applicable to upper school or university courses in English literature. The book also contains a wide enough variety of practical language activities to aid the language development of the advanced learner who may not otherwise be concerned with the study of literature.

Cassette

The book is accompanied by a cassette which is an essential part of the course. Listening to texts read by different people offers the learner a valuable extra perspective on the texts and their interpretation. The cassette should be used with all parts of the book where the text is recorded, and not only where it is specifically stated in the instructions. The texts which are read on the cassette are marked by the symbol 📼 .

Metalanguage

Metalanguage and technical terms are kept to a minimum. Some specialised terminology does, however, occur when effects need to be described economically. For learners, metalanguage and terminology must not become ends in themselves. Understanding the concept is much more important than remembering terminology.

Visual and aural stimuli

The book contains a small number of pictures intended to stimulate thought and discussion on the themes and content of the texts they accompany. Teachers are encouraged to use additional pictures, music, pre-reading activities, or other aids and stimuli, as appropriate. These should be used as widely as possible to put the learner into a receptive frame of mind before approaching a text, and to provide a basis on which discussion and analysis of language can develop.

Use of mother tongue

At the teacher's discretion certain pair and group work activities may be conducted in the learners' mother tongue if such discussion facilitates appreciation of a text which might otherwise not have occurred. The individual teacher must judge when, and for how long, mother tongue discussion should take place. It is nevertheless intended that teachers encourage the use of English whenever possible.

The texts

We have selected a wide range of texts from different historical periods of English literature. Our main aims are to choose texts on a variety of themes, to use poetry, prose and drama, and to include complete texts where possible. We have also devoted one unit (Unit 10) to a text of 10,000 words (a short story by Somerset Maugham). We consider this to be a rare advantage in a literature study book, since such works tend to rely too much on short texts and extracts.

A further aim is to represent different types of literary work within the three main genres of poetry, prose and drama. This is particularly import-ant because some literary conventions and forms are specific to Western literature, and learners from other cultures will need to have access to them. A large number of the texts are from the twentieth century. This does not, however, guarantee that learners will find modern literature more comprehensible than literature from previous centuries, even though the language may appear superficially 'easier'.

Finally, there is no strict interpretation of the term 'English literature'. If we were to restrict this to the British Isles, we would have to ignore texts written in English in other parts of the world and those translated into English. Such texts form part of the experience of writers and readers of 'English Literature' and are in themselves eminently suitable for an integrated approach to the study of English language and literature.

The teacher's role

The role of the teacher using this book is to facilitate, stimulate and support in activities where learners investigate, explore and interpret literary texts. The process is learner-centred, and the book allows few opportunities for teacher exposition. The teacher is required to involve learners with the text, encourage them to support a viewpoint using the evidence provided by the writer's use of language, and to make initial responses to and judgements about the text. The learners then have the opportunity to share their experiences, argue their opinions, and try to appreciate other people's positions, even if they do not agree with them. Sometimes these discussions are extended to writing, thus providing an individual task, in contrast to the group-centred activities. There is specific guidance for each unit in Section III of the Teacher's Book.

The Teacher's Book is not intended as a list of questions and answers for every text. It contains possible questions. We recommend that you should accept all suggested answers, and use them as a basis for brief discussion. If you wish to refute an answer do so with reference to the text.

Reinforcement of language and literature

This is not a course in literary criticism. The book is designed to show learners that there are many productive ways in which literature and language can reinforce each other. Language-based activities can lead on to higher order skills such as interpretation, evaluation, and also to literary contextual awareness. To achieve this, the correct balance must be struck between language studies and literature studies: language and literature cannot, and should not, be mutually exclusive domains. This book, therefore, may be used to supplement both language courses and literature courses. The learner who can express his or her own attitudes, feelings, and experiences with ease and fluency has attained a very high level of competence. This book is designed to take the learner some steps along the way towards that goal by presenting literary texts as self-contained, authentic and intrinsically motivating language material, which can extend experience and encourage the use of language.

General design of the units

We hope that classes will work through the ten units in the book more or less in sequence, since the 'approaches' are to some extent cumulative. However, each unit is also largely self-contained, so that teachers can select any single unit for study.

Each unit follows the same general design. There are five main parts:

The *Introduction to the student* states the purpose of each unit, thus providing the learner with a focus.

The *Orientation* section prepares the learner for work on the main texts of each unit. It introduces and practises some of the techniques associated with the 'approach'. This may involve work on non-literary as well as literary text. Much of general value can be learned by studying the two together.

Sections I, II, III etc. are designed to exploit the language of selected texts. Where possible learners are introduced to the different texts in ways which will develop a fuller understanding, helping them to empathise with the writer's intent.

Most units have sections entitled *Exploitation* which extend the work done on a particular text, and encourage the learner to return to that text to develop a deeper understanding of it.

The summary of the unit serves to remind the learner of the main points that have emerged in that unit.

Fast route

If there is sufficient class time and you cannot cover all the texts in the book, we suggest you follow our fast route rather than limiting learners to certain units and working right through them. The scheme allows for study of only two or three texts per unit (instead of the average of five), and ensures that learners are introduced to the whole range of 'approaches' which are a feature of the book. Teachers should note that the key texts in each unit are generally those which receive particular attention in the Teacher's Book.

Unit 1	Section A	
	Orientation	'Expert aims to salvage détente from ocean bed'
	Summary I	'Cat in the Rain'
	Section B	
	Prediction II	*The History of Mr. Polly* (extract)
Unit 2	*Orientation*	'Meeting at Night'
	Scenario IV	*Great Expectations* (extract)
Unit 3	*Ranking IV*	'Snake'
Unit 4	*Reading aloud I*	'The General'
	Reading aloud VI	*The Prime of Miss Jean Brodie* (extract)
Unit 5	Section A	
	Language patterns I	'Spacepoem 3: Off Course'
	Section B	
	Exploitation	Creative writing models
Unit 6	Section A	
	Vocabulary I	'The Eagle'
	Section B	
	Vocabulary III	*A Very Private Life* (extract)
Unit 7	*Discourse III*	'Malaysia'
Unit 8	*Stylistic analysis I*	'Futility'
Unit 9	*Background IV*	'After the Battle'
Unit 10	*Forum III*	'The Force of Circumstance'

Re-cycled texts

Teachers may also find it useful to know that the following texts appear
in more than one unit. To supplement the 'fast route' above, it is possible
to study certain texts from the perspective of more than one approach
(see also Section IV *Combining the approaches*).

Texts	*Units*
'Cat in the Rain'	1, 10
'The General'	4, 9
'After the Battle'	4, 9
'The Eagle'	5, 6, 8
'Meeting at Night'	2, 5
Lady Chatterley's Lover (extract)	6, 7
'The Force of Circumstance'	7, 9, 10

Section II   Preparing the learner to use 'The Web of Words'

If learners have never previously studied literature in the ways indicated in this book their initial reaction may be one of puzzlement. Some learners ask questions such as 'Why are we doing this?' or 'What is the purpose of this exercise?' Though each unit has an introduction which attempts to answer the latter question, learners will benefit from an initial briefing, which takes an overview of the book and the process which it incorporates.

The following points are not intended for presentation to learners 'in a block', but as appropriate during the course, or at the start of a lesson, or when changing from one type of exercise to another.

1 Literature is also language. The book recognises this, and you will spend a lot of time looking at language. The purpose of this is to find out what constitutes literature, and, hopefully, to see the text's 'value'.

2 Another way of looking at the language/literature duality is that first you are trying to find out how a text works, and what its particular meanings are. Then you will try to appreciate that text by finding what it has to say to you.

3 When dealing with prose, in particular, you will be dealing with parts of texts. But it is hoped that you will find the part stimulating, and want to read the whole text as soon as a chance arises.

4 'Appreciating' a literary text usually implies enjoying that text. The more you enjoy a text the more you will want to read of the same author, or of the same type or 'genre'. But as a serious student of literature you must also learn to explain your response with direct reference to features of the text. To do this you will need language, though not necessarily literary language. It is hoped that your language competence, both spoken and written, will improve as you use this book.

5 In the past, 'response' to literature has very often been someone else's response, either the teacher's, or someone accepted by him or her as an authority. This book is much more interested in your response. You will frequently be invited to work in pairs or small groups to put together a response by finding out if you agree or disagree with other

learners. In this way you will build up meaning by interacting with the text and then with each other.

6 The book uses a certain amount of linguistic terminology or 'meta-language'. These terms are often used to avoid an unnecessarily lengthy explanation. You should, of course, try to understand the concept to which the term applies, but the book is not concerned with getting you to memorise any special literary technical terms.

7 The book includes texts from different periods of English literature, and different kinds of poetry, prose and drama from within those periods. Modern (that is twentieth century) writers predominate, which should help to some extent where students of literature are also students of language.

8 Unit 9 is devoted to background, and attempts to show how some texts, more than others, relate to the context in which they were produced. This is perhaps a more conventional approach to literary study. In this book you will spend more time looking at the language. But this does not mean that you should ignore the background, where it is important.

Section III   The units

1   What's going on?
Summary and narrative prediction

Part A   Notes

Aims

The purpose of this unit is to show learners how useful it is (a) in the course of their reading to produce *predictions* of how they think a narrative will develop, and (b) after they have read a text, to write a *summary* of it.

The Approach

In *The Web of Words* learners are regularly asked to produce summaries of what they have read. These are usually straightforward accounts of 'what happens' in the text. Such a summary can give learners a 'way in' to understanding a text. It often provides a 'prose gloss' which is preliminary to further study and leads to fuller understanding. Writing a summary within an approximate word limit is also a practical linguistic task which can help learners to develop their ability to manipulate language structures.

Predicting 'what happens next' in a text is related to summary in that it is necessary first to make a mental summary of 'the plot so far' before a reasonable prediction can be made.

Prediction is a natural reading activity, but if a text does not provide us with an immediately recognisable frame of reference, we have difficulty in assessing what is going to be significant in what we have read. Thus prediction is better suited to clearly plotted narrative than to, say, lyric poems. The fact that the most interesting plots are unpredictable or difficult to predict, makes the exercise a challenging and illuminating one.

Summaries, too, are best suited to narratives and accounts of 'what happens'. It is essential that the learner should realise that a summary of what happens in a literary text can never convey its essential meaning and destroys the style of the text. This is particularly true of 'Cat in the Rain' (see Student's Book pp. 6–9) where what happens in the surface narrative line bears little relation to what can be 'read between the lines'. This is best illustrated by comparison with non-literary text, where summaries more accurately preserve the meaning. Summary should not be used on literary text as an end in itself, but as a strategy which provides a basis for valuable insights.

Techniques

Learners should be encouraged to make a prediction and then substantiate it with a formula such as:

'I suggested . . . because it says . . . in line . . . '

A useful initial stage is 'brainstorming'. Learners think of as many developments as possible. Their suggestions are noted and open discussion on the relative merits of the different predictions follows. It is more interesting if apparently bizarre suggestions are not rejected without discussion, providing, of course, that they have some connection with the text.

This activity lends itself to group work. Groups should reach consensus on the most suitable prediction and then compare their version with those of other groups. This activity produces heightened interest in and involvement with the text, as groups and individuals read on into the text and check whether their expectations are confirmed or not.

Part B   Texts for intensive study

1   'Cat in the Rain': Ernest Hemingway

Summary and prediction do not, of course, exhaust the texts used. 'Cat in the Rain' particularly, as a complete short story, merits more intensive study.

The following questions can be answered from close study of the text.
a) Why do you think the American wife is interested in the cat?
    To relieve her boredom.
b) When the husband says 'Don't get wet' (l. 27) how does he feel about his wife?
    He is not very interested in what she does but feels the need to say something.
c) Why does the wife like the hotel owner?
    He shows interest and concern.
d) How does George react when his wife tells him the cat is gone?
    He shows interest briefly, then starts reading again.
e) Which words show that George easily gets impatient with his wife?
    'Oh, shut up and get something to read.' (l. 101)

The following questions are for open discussion.
f) In what way is the setting/orientation of the opening paragraph important to the story?
g) 'The wife seems to be nervous and tense.' Do you agree with this view?
h) Do you consider the wife provokes George with her seemingly impetuous behaviour?
i) What importance does the maid have in the story?
j) Is there any significance in the title 'Cat in the Rain' (rather than 'a cat' or 'the cat')?

2 *The History of Mr. Polly*: H. G. Wells

The title of the book from which this extract is taken suggests both a society or social structure, and a period. As it is not anticipated that learners will read the whole book, it would perhaps be useful to investigate these areas.

The following questions can be answered from close study of the text. (Do not insist on answers exactly the same as those given.)
a) What is Mr Polly's 'double life'?
   He is looking for a job, and is looking for something romantic.
b) How do we know that Mr Polly is not very serious about getting a job?
   He only talks about getting a job.
c) What is the limit of Mr Polly's ambitions?
   To own a shop in London, or, possibly to work in a smart London shop.
d) Why is Mr Polly enthusiastic about 'the idea of property'?
   It would give him social importance, and hopefully wealth.
e) Why does Mr Polly cycle out into the countryside (ll. 40–52)?
   He is determined not to waste time with friends or relatives.

Collate the information about Mr Polly on the board or on an overhead projector. Write the headings on the left and get the learners to suggest answers.

Mr Polly

Residence .... lodges with the Johnson family
Present job ....
Economic status ....
Age ....
Marital status ....
Educational background ....
Interests...................................

Ask the learners, with reference to their answers, to classify Mr Polly in their own society, and at the present.

Example:

i) A charming young gentleman. Has enough money to live comfortably. Intelligent. Sociable and well-liked.

ii) Unemployed. Lives on social benefits. No prospects. Lacks 'drive' or energy.

Note that there is further exploitation of this text in Unit 3 Part C.

2 Scenario: Language, dialogue and setting

Part A   Notes

Aims

The pedagogic considerations in this unit are to encourage learners (a) to look at a text as a whole, which is an important preparation for any later critical studies or exercises, and (b) to overcome their concern with specific lexical items. Non-native speakers commonly 'get stuck' with low-frequency lexis which is not essential to an understanding of the text.

The Approach

This 'approach', though very simple, seems to have been relatively little used in literature teaching either with native or non-native speakers. The learners are required to put themselves in the position of director or producer of a film or videotape. They must take all the decisions. This can be used as the sole approach to a text, or as a supplement to any other approach where it is intended to dramatise a text. It is creative, requiring visualisation, and can only be done, of course, with close examination of the text itself. The learner must examine the text for clues. In this respect, it is a focusing technique, and is particularly demanding when applied to poetry or prose extracts, which do not carry stage directions.

Certain texts lend themselves to this 'approach' better than others; action is better than thought; interaction better than soliloquising; movement better than stillness; prose or drama better than poetry.

Techniques

Actual production experience is neither expected nor required. Learners are required only to make suggestions for a 'scenario', and then to discuss in groups. Group work is an integral part of this approach. Members of the group must, of course, justify their suggestions by reference to the text, and should attempt to reach some sort of consensus (see the ranking exercises in Unit 3). The process can, if so desired, be completely out of

15

the hands of the teacher, though the latter should always be ready to point out clues in the text, which learners may have overlooked.

The first text is worked out in detail (pp. 21–2). This should be studied carefully before proceeding to other texts.

Part B Texts for intensive study

1 *Last to Go*: Harold Pinter

This play is likely to be seen as 'different' or 'unusual' by even the weakest learners. This means in effect that learners are reacting to it, and this should be fully exploited. Do not attempt to teach or to ask questions about the play before the 'scenario' exercise in the Student's Book has been completed. If it generates puzzlement do not attempt to clarify everything. There is no need to resort to lecture. Keep all options open.

Begin with the questions in the Student's Book (p. 29). Keep these questions as 'open' as possible. Do not indicate that any specific answer is correct.

Continue with these literal and inferential questions. (Allow only very brief answers.)
a) What is the grammar error in line 1?
b) What is meant by a 'bit of trade'?
c) What newspapers does the man sell?
d) What is unusual about the phrase 'like a shot' in this context?
e) What time of night does the conversation take place?
f) Who is George?
g) Did the newspaper seller really go to Victoria to find George?
Extend this list.

Do not 'work through' the following questions. Encourage longer answers and try to find one which provokes discussion. Keep discussion open to the point where a learner makes a value judgement. For example:
    'This play is silly/nonsense/boring.'
    'This play is interesting/puzzling/realistic.'
Take up any such judgement. Ask the class if they agree or disagree by a show of hands. Where there are conflicting opinions ask learners to defend their viewpoint. Cross reference to Unit 10 *Forum*, but for this play do not ask learners to argue a case which they do not feel.
h) Do you think this conversation is more, or less, like 'real life' than other plays that you know?
i) Do you think this conversation would be of any interest to a theatre audience? Why (not)?
j) Do you consider this play 'dramatic'? If so, in what way?

k) Do you think this play is entertaining? If so, is it because of the characters, the situation, the unresolved mystery of George, or because of anything else?

2 *Great Expectations*: Charles Dickens (first extract)

At least part of this text should be studied as a contrast to *Last to Go* above. *Last to Go* is drama, while the opening chapter of *Great Expectations* is prose narrative. It could, however, easily be argued that here the prose narrative is a great deal more dramatic than the drama. The 'approach' (i.e. guided discussion, with the task of making an imaginary film) should reveal the dramatic element and increase the learners' understanding of the author's narrative technique. The characteristics of this technique can be described in simple terms as:

a) the use of a narrator;

b) density of words;

c) a great amount of detail;

d) sentence construction which would be rare, or very unusual, in spoken language. For example:

'My first most vivid and broad impression of the identity of things . . . ' (l. 24)

Use this as a starting point for the contrastive study. Elicit from learners the virtual 'opposites' in the Pinter text. Encourage any further comment which contrasts the two texts but consider also the following:

e) use of free reported speech in prose narrative. See *Great Expectations* line 70:

'I earnestly expressed my hope that he wouldn't.'

What did Pip actually say? Learners should find other examples of this technique. Ask them to offer an opinion as to why it is used.

f) Suggest to learners that MAN in *Last to Go* is from the same social class as 'the terrible stranger' in *Great Expectations*. Elicit opinions on whether their language is similar or different. (It is similar, but the stranger has a much more urgent need to communicate.)

Dickens' style, and in particular the great amount of detail mentioned above, lends itself to large numbers of 'closed' questions. For example:

How did Pip know his family name was Pirrip? (l. 5)

What was the name of Pip's sister? (l. 6)

Who had she married? (l. 7)

etc.

As this looks only at phrases or sentences, and not at the discourse, it is not very useful. Ask students to make a few such questions, and point out that unless they draw attention to some particular feature which might be important, the questions only break the text into lists of unrelated details.

Instead of this, break the text into separate sections, as follows:

lines 1–4   Pip introduces himself
lines 5–22   Pip's family background
lines 23–37   An afternoon visit to the churchyard
lines 38–40   Threat from a stranger

This of course is a form of summary, but do not use the word 'summary' for the process. Get learners to label each section or incident with a caption of between two and six words. Point out that these sections will not always correspond to paragraphs as above. Complete this to line 72, and invite individuals to indicate the place where they mark the breaks, and the captions. Allow discussion and differences of opinion unless you consider a caption is decidedly 'wrong'.

If time allows ask learners to do a similar breakdown for the second extract as homework, and follow it up briefly in the next lesson.

Part C   Further exploitation

Last to Go

Ask learners to improvise a conversation between the BARMAN and an educated customer (a lawyer / a bank manager). Begin:

MAN: Not very busy at present eh? I suppose it gets a bit busier later, does it?

BARMAN: Oh yes. Trade's usually fairly brisk about ten. (Continue for about ten responses. Try to keep the character of the barman as close to Pinter's as possible.)

Learners are not re-writing styles (see Unit 7) in this exploitation, which is intended as an oral exercise. But ask them to consider, very briefly, how their style and Pinter's differ.

Great Expectations

Learners re-write lines 38–54 as a homework exercise, but this time the person who surprises Pip is the vicar of the church. Begin:
    'My dear little fellow!' cried a concerned voice.
Again learners are not re-writing styles but, as in *Last to Go* above, changing the 'dramatis personae'. Ask learners to consider, very briefly, how their style and Dickens' differ.

Note that there are suggestions for further exploitation of *Last to Go* and *Macbeth* in Unit 3 Part C.

3 Talking together: Ranking

Part A Notes

Aims

The main purpose of this unit is to encourage learners to discuss their impressions, ideas and feelings about a literary text.

The Approach

Ranking is an exercise in which a number of statements are made about a text, and then learners must put them into order of importance. These 'statements' may be either interpretations of the text, or details of the action (if any), or value judgements on characters, though different types of statement should not be mixed, otherwise it is impossible to rank them. The task is for learners to rank the interpretations, details, value judgements from most important to least important. To do so, of course, requires a close correlation of statement with text, though as opinions are involved there can be no single correct answer.

All statements for consideration and ranking should be reasonable, and therefore, in theory, capable of being ranked first. They are not 'distractors', as in the procedure for multiple choice questions.

Techniques

This 'approach' is particularly suited to group work. We suggest the following general classroom procedure, though variations are at the discretion of the teacher.

1 Work through the text using any 'approach' or combination of 'approaches' from this book, other than ranking.
2 Present the statements to be ranked. Ask each learner to make his or her own selection of at least statements one to five in order of import- ance. A longer list is possible, but one to twelve, for example, is difficult to correlate.
3 Divide into groups of seven or eight. Each group must reach consensus

on the order of importance of, again, statements one to five, or a longer list. Discussion should be in English where possible, and the ranking should always be referred to the text, not to generalised opinion. Be careful with time allotment for this step; too lengthy discussion will lead to boredom, too short, to frustration.

4 If time allows, the full class reconvenes and attempts to reach consensus as a whole. This step can also be attempted very usefully after an interval of a few days, or the following week (where practicable) where interest is revived, and a useful second glance given to the text.

Note that this 'approach' is heavily learner-orientated. After step 1 above, which should not take too long, the teacher has only a monitoring role, and all the work, including investigation of the text, is done by the learners themselves. For this reason the teacher should avoid a 'correct' ranking, and let the general consensus (4 above) stand, even if he or she disagrees personally.

Part B Texts for intensive study

1 'An Irish Airman Foresees his Death': W. B. Yeats

Read out the brief introductory notes to this poem in the Student's Book (p. 45).

The following questions are arranged in pairs. The first question in each pair leads on to a more 'open' question. (Answers are given for the 'closed' questions only.)

a) i) Who is the narrator?
      An Irish airman.
   ii) Who is he speaking to?
b) i) What does 'fate' in line 1 refer to?
      The narrator's death.
   ii) What word in the poem contrasts most markedly with the 'fate' of line 1?
      Delight.
c) i) Who does 'them' in line 7 refer to?
      The Irish (Kiltartan's poor).
   ii) What is the narrator's attitude towards his countrymen?
d) i) How do you explain the word 'lonely' in line 11?
      Something personal and private, but nevertheless important.
   ii) Do you think the poet is making any statement about war? If so, what?
e) i) What is 'this tumult in the clouds'?

Presumably a contest ('a dog fight') with another military aero-plane.
ii) How would you explain the 'tumult' in the narrator's mind?

2 'Snake': D. H. Lawrence

The Student's Book offers a summary (32 words) of the last 40 lines of the poem (p. 53). Ask the learners to re-write it and incorporate it into a 65-word summary of the whole poem. Consider one or two completed summaries and consider their adequacy, or otherwise, as summaries. What has been left out that might have been put in? What are the important points that cannot be omitted? How can they be joined together in effective summary writing?

Then invite comment and discussion on the following questions.
a) It is easy to make a summary of 'Snake'. Why?
b) Can a summary capture the effect of this poem?
Invite general response and accept any reasonable answers. Allow plenty of time for topic (b) to develop. Prompt if necessary with 'Would you say that . . . ?' type stimuli. Make a check-list of possible points. For example:
– The poet uses extensive detail to describe the setting.
– The poet creates an atmosphere more than he tells a story.
– The poet is concerned with attitudes – his own and others' – and summary is not suited to capture this.
etc.

No question sequence is suggested for this text as the three-part ranking exercise elicits and ranks 'impressions' which are inevitably similar to the answers to 'open' questions. The preamble to the poem (Student's Book p. 50) says 'the poem is loosely structured and has some of the features of prose'. There are nevertheless marked poetic words/phrases, and the lesson should focus on these.
a) Select three or four such phrases and 'analyse' how they differ from non-poetic discourse (see also Unit 7). For example:
    'trailed his yellow-brown slackness' (l. 8)
    'Slackness' is not normally applied to snakes.
    'Trailed' and 'slackness' indicate the smooth, quiet movement.
    Compare 'earth-brown, earth-golden' (l. 20) with 'yellow-brown'.
    Other words/phrases for comment:
    'sipped' (l. 11)
    'like a second comer' (l. 15)
    'drinking, as cattle do' / 'as drinking cattle do' (ll. 16/17) (repetition)
b) Invite learners to select three such phrases from the poem and analyse / comment on them first with another learner and if called upon to do

so to the class. In doing so they are in fact answering an 'open' question of the type:

'What is special about the phrase . . . ?'

With advanced learners look again at the last twelve lines of the poem. Elicit the tone of the poem (moralising?). Find phrases which support this view. Then ask the 'open' questions:
– Do you accept this or do you find it tedious?
– What would be the effect if the poem finished at the line:

'Writhed like lightning, and was gone'?

Note that this poem is particularly suitable for reading aloud using the variables from Unit 4.

There is further exploitation of this poem in Unit 8 Part C where learners are asked to compare it with Emily Dickinson's 'A narrow Fellow in the Grass'.

Part C   Further exploitation

Return to the extract from *The History of Mr. Polly* (Unit 1) and ask learners to make 6–8 statements about Mr Polly which would make a reasonable ranking exercise. Then ask them to exchange statements with another learner in the group and do each other's exercises.

Further tasks might involve making a ranking exercise for a drama text. Pinter's *Last to Go* and the extract from *Macbeth* (Unit 2) would make good starting points.

4 Read it aloud: Text and phonology

Part A Notes

Aims

This unit is designed to help learners to appreciate the sound patterns the writer has created. It will also give learners the opportunity to develop the oral expression of their interpretation of the text.

The Approach

Everyone knows that the words of a play only 'come alive' when they are spoken. The way in which they are spoken is a combination of the actor's skill and the director's instruction and interpretation. 'How they are spoken' also makes the greater part of the difference between a competent performance and a brilliant one, although there are of course other non-linguistic features involved, such as the staging (see Unit 2) and physical movement.

'How the words are spoken' is a complex subject. The actors and the general reader probably both have an idea of how they would articulate the words on the page before they actually do so. The native speaker intuitively imagines a certain way of reading to suit the text, especially with drama and poetry.

The process of imagining the sound and reading aloud does, however, need training, particularly among non-native speakers. Some of the variables listed in the Student's Book will, of course, operate in all languages, but while the native speaker can give these his or her full attention, the foreign learner is probably concerned with lexical, or syntactic, or cohesion problems, in addition to these articulatory difficulties.

An example will probably make this clear. Read the following, which is two stanzas of light verse by Robert Louis Stevenson.

From a Railway Carriage

FASTER than fairies, faster than witches,
Bridges and houses, hedges and ditches;
And charging along like troops in a battle,
All through the meadows the horses and cattle:
All of the sights of the hill and the plain   5
Fly as thick as driving rain;
And ever again, in the wink of an eye,
Painted stations whistle by.

Here is a child who clambers and scrambles,
All by himself, and gathering brambles;   10
Here is a tramp who stands and gazes;
And there is the green for stringing the daisies!
Here is a cart run away in the road
Lumping along with man and load;
And here is a mill and there is a river: 15
Each a glimpse and gone for ever!

Robert Louis Stevenson

This poem illustrates the tempo variable (quick–slow) particularly
clearly. Now listen to the recorded reading of 'From a Railway Carriage'
(at the end of the cassette) and use it to exemplify this to the learners.

The section in the Student's Book marked 'Orientation' (p. 54) should
also be 'worked through' before commencing any of the texts in this
'approach'.

Part B   Texts for intensive study

1   'Youth': Joseph Conrad

This passage describes the sinking of a ship, told reflectively, years later,
by one of the crew. In spite of the brilliance of the writing, however, the
event is restrained, and lacking in drama. There is none of the turmoil
which you might associate with the sinking of a ship. This gives the
possibility of an interesting multiple choice question as a starting point.

The 'restrained description' of the sinking of the *Judea* is because:
i)   the story is told at a distance in time;
ii)   the crew recognised it as inevitable – the fire had been burning for
      days;
iii) Conrad wants to minimise human feelings and describe the sinking
      objectively;
iv)   the weather was calm;

v)   the scene was in its way beautiful; disorder and turmoil would spoil the beauty of the scene.

Give learners as much information about the complete story as they might need to select one of the above (there is of course no single correct answer). Ask learners to indicate their choice by show of hands, and then ask some to justify their choice. This cannot be done entirely by reference to this extract; in other words learners must use their imagination.

The text is explicit. Its force is in the lines themselves, not in 'reading between the lines' (compare 'Cat in the Rain' Unit 1). Two features stand out. The first is the lists or alternatives:
    'A high clear flame, an immense and lonely flame . . . '
This is investigated in the Student's Book on page 62, numbers 3, 4 and 5. Make sure that learners attempt an answer to number 4. Ask them if this technique produces an effect similar to or different from the detail in Dickens' *Great Expectations* (used for intensive study in Unit 2).
Suggested answer: It is different. The author is not so much giving detail as using a device for holding our attention.
It may help learners to understand this concept if you compare it to the process of playing a video tape and holding one picture as 'a still', to ensure its impact.
    The second important feature of the text is its discourse structure, or the way in which it coheres. Every phrase or clause is closely linked to at least one other part of the text. Consider:
    the boats (l. 2)   the men (l. 3)   the oars (l. 19)   the long boat (l. 20)
    we pulled across her stern (l. 21)

or

    ship (l. 4)
        ↖
      flame (l. 8)
          ↖
        smoke (l. 9)
            ↖
          burned (l. 10)
              ↘
            funeral pile (l. 10)

Numerous other 'links' can be made in this second 'chain'. To change the metaphor: ask learners to make a discourse map, circling words in different sentences and joining them together by drawing lines in pencil.

Note that these 'joining lines' can refer both backwards and forwards. Thus 'masts' (l. 15) links with 'ship' (l. 4) 'she' (l. 22) and 'stern' (l. 23).

Note that there is further work on word links in the Student's Book in Unit 6 Section C *Orientation: Lexical chains*.

2 *The Prime of Miss Jean Brodie*: Muriel Spark

Re-read the brief introduction to this text on page 62 of the Student's Book. Then ask the following inferential questions. (Possible answers are given. These are not the only answers. Encourage other answers, and do not read out these answers if the learners provide reasonable answers.)

a) Who are the 'intruders' referred to by Miss Brodie?
    The headmistress, other teachers, an inspector, anybody who was opposed to Miss Brodie.

b) Re-read the paragraph beginning 'Meantime I will tell you about my last summer holiday in Egypt.'
    What does this suggest about the character of Miss Brodie?
    She is an unorthodox teacher. She lives in a world of fantasy. She is a romantic.

c) What is implied by 'Miss Brodie . . . stood erect . . . staring out of the window like Joan of Arc'?
    She was a leader. She thought of herself as a leader.

d) Why is Miss Brodie so concerned with her 'prime'?
    She wants to impress her pupils.

e) What does Miss Brodie probably mean by 'You must then live it to the full'?
    She will do what she thinks right. She will not accept arbitrary constraints.

f) What is unusual in the way Miss Brodie talks to the children?
    She talks to them as if they were considerably older than ten or eleven.

By working through the above six questions an impression of Miss Brodie should emerge. This is that she is strange or eccentric in an amusing way. From this the learners should be able to see the comic features of the text. Do not 'explain' these. Ask learners to identify amusing features, for example, the use of the word 'intruders' to describe anyone who came to her outdoor lesson. Do not try to exhaust the humour of the text. Suggest frequent re-reading at intervals, after the intensive study.

Ask learners to read the whole of Chapters 1 and 2 if practicable.

Part C Further exploitation

Lawrence's 'Snake' (Unit 3 *Ranking IV*) would make a very good text for reading aloud using the variables from this unit.

5 'On the inside': Writing and patterns of language

Part A Notes

Aims

This unit builds on the largely thematic approaches of Units 1, 2 and 3 but is the first to adopt an explicitly stylistic approach. The aim is to help learners to recognise some of the literary effects produced by certain features of language. In this unit there will be a concentration on grammar though it is, of course, impossible to divorce effects produced by grammar from those brought about by other patterns of language such as phonetic and lexical patterns. Unit 6 is devoted to vocabulary and Unit 4 to sound features, so these will not be our main concern here; but, in order to emphasise the point concerning the overlap of language features, which is particularly apparent in literary texts, learners will be asked to consider the overlap of grammar and graphology, that is, the patterns made by the words on the printed page.

The Approach

To aid appreciation of simple and complex grammatical patterns learners will be asked to practise exercises to which we have given the term *elastic sentences*. This can involve breaking down long sentences into simpler units and combining sentences into longer and more complex structures. Thus the learner is asked to experience stylistic patterns from the *inside* as a result of his or her own writing.

Techniques

In this unit learners are also strongly encouraged to write their own poetry and prose, using some of the structures and patterns of the texts they have studied as models or starting points. It is a very good way of understanding how literary texts are put together and what some of the problems are. It is a way of encountering directly the *process* of writing.

The unit becomes progressively learner-centred, concluding with further 'patterns' for learners' own writing.

Creative writing in EFL

It is not an easy task to encourage learners to write their own poetry. Often learners are inhibited because they are writing in a foreign language, are afraid they will not do it 'right', or are simply unaccustomed to such writing tasks. It is important to recognise and to help learners to recognise that it is not a case of 'right' or 'wrong' and that language can be used ungrammatically if a particular effect needs to be created. Poems are not 'corrected' for their language; it is a matter of choosing the right words for the job. It is therefore helpful to encourage learners to write two or three 'drafts' or versions of the poem – perhaps over a longer period of time than one 'lesson' – before they decide it is how they want it. We must also recognise here that the patterns of language suggested are very simple in structure and that they are only a foundation upon which the poem is built. However, it will help learners to understand the discipline needed in all creative and imaginative writing, particularly in the early stages of their writing, if they are told that they must follow these 'rules', however uncomplicated they are. As we have seen, simple patterns can be used for very interesting effects. For learners who really lack the linguistic confidence to perform these tasks, we have found that things might be made easier if the teacher:

a) supplies a title for the poem and/or
b) supplies a first line and/or
c) gives a number of suggested words for use in the poem in advance.

With learners who need direction in what they are to write about, it can be useful to use the stimulus of a picture, a piece of music, a photograph, a newspaper article etc.

If you feel it is appropriate to your class, learners may be asked to read each other's poems and discuss their reactions to them.

Part B   Text for intensive study

'Spacepoem 3: Off Course': Edwin Morgan

The following questions can be answered through interpretation of the text.

a) Why is the seat **weightless** (l. 1)?
    Lack of gravity in space.
b) What is the 'orbit wisecrack' (l. 4)?
    Jokes cracked by astronauts as they orbit the earth.

c) Why is the mouth-organ **smuggled** (l. 5)?
Astronauts would probably be forbidden to take musical instruments on board with them.
d) What are the 'crawling deltas' (l. 9)?
The mouths of several rivers running into ths sea. Seen from a great height it might look as if the rivers were crawling like spiders.
e) Why is the headphone **crackling** (l. 11)?
Because of the great distance between the spaceship and the earth which would affect radio reception and cause crackling noises.
f) Why is the moon **growing** (l. 14)?
It seems to be getting larger as it comes closer.
g) What is **debris** (l. 17)?
Lots of damaged articles and objects usually caused as the result of an accident.
h) What is 'the floating song' (l. 21)?
Songs sung or music played by the astronauts which is now a series of sound waves floating off into eternal space.

Pay particular attention to *Language Patterns I* question 8 and the pairings of listed words. For example:
i) What is the connection between **pitch black** (*normal collocation referring to the night sky outside the cabin*) **pitch velvet** and **pitch sleep** (*more unusual collocations, the latter suggesting death*)?
j) Why is the smuggled mouth-organ now in an **orbit** of its own? And why is the headphone now **weightless**?
k) Why is there debris **inside** the cabin?
l) What is the condition of a man whose beard **crackles** (l. 20)?
Icy-cold, probably dead.

Part C   Further exploitation

Although the Edwin Morgan poem is entitled 'Spacepoem' learners might be encouraged to think of other analogies. The somewhat random list of mental impressions could, for example, suggest mental disorientation with the idea of a space journey standing for a journey into a darkness of insanity. Alternatively, the more striking and poetic images from line 15 onwards might suggest a consciousness which becomes more original, creative and 'on course' the more it goes off course from a conventional direction. Very open questions here.

6 Words and their impact: Structures of vocabulary

Part A Notes

Aims

The purpose of this unit is to develop strategies in the learner for interpreting lexical items and to encourage sensitivity to the way writers use words to create literary effects.

The Approach

This is the second of the units devoted to a consideration of the stylistic features of a text. Here we pay particular attention to the structure and organisation of lexis. Learners are introduced to the idea of semantic fields and word families, and to the way in which writers can exploit such relations to produce 'metaphoric' effects. Another basic idea we introduce is that of collocation (word partnerships) and the way poets play with our expectations of how words usually combine with one another. Finally, learners consider the way words combine grammatically and structurally to ensure the cohesion of a text.

Techniques

One main teaching technique used here is gap-filling, a less rigorously applied version of standard cloze procedure. This procedure is used flexibly so that learners will be practising gap-filling exercises to enhance their awareness of how collocational and structural semantic patterns relate to the creation of particular literary effects. The technique also aids recognition of the cohesive patterns made by grammatical and lexical words. Teachers may find it useful to practise the gap-filling exercises first on non-literary text where a different order of complexity is in operation. The teacher might, for example, introduce a standard cloze procedure of deleting every eighth word of a basic text which may even be known to the learners (perhaps even one in their own language) in order to acquaint them with the technique and to give them practice. We have deleted words which are, in the first place, lexically significant but the technique can be used to draw attention to other features of language structure and organisation.

Word association and word families are explored principally by means of *scales*, with learners regularly being asked to assess the 'power' of words in relation to each other along a scale of 1–10 or 1–5.

Part B Texts for intensive study

1 'The Eagle': Alfred Lord Tennyson

Questions could focus on the physical characteristics of the eagle and then lead on to more demanding questions on what the eagle might be said to represent. The questions in the Student's Book (pp. 84–5) concentrate on particular lexical items which help with answers relating to both physical and symbolic qualities. (For example, the use of the word **hand** suggests that we are meant to conceive of the eagle as more than just a bird; **mountain** and **wall** together might suggest that natural and human/domestic worlds merge in the eagle?)

a) Why does the eagle inhabit **lonely** lands?
    The remoteness and distance of the eagle is stressed.
b) Why is the eagle 'ring'd with the azure world'?
    It suggests the power of the eagle as he surveys the world from a great height.
c) Why is the sea **wrinkled**?
    This again suggests the height of the eagle. From a distance the movements of the surface of the sea might resemble wrinkles on the skin.
d) What impression is created by ' . . . like a thunderbolt he falls'?
    Again a sense of power and danger is created by the eagle.

The following questions are for open discussion.
e) Why is the subtitle of the poem 'Fragment'?
f) Does the eagle represent a 'bold, free and independent spirit'?
g) Why is there no argumentation in the poem? Why is there just a series of asserted actions?
h) What state of mind in a human being is suggested by the description of the eagle? Would you agree with critics who say that this is a fragment of the mind of an apocalyptic poet?

2 *A Very Private Life*: Michael Frayn

Begin by asking and discussing these questions.
a) What kind of stories begin with 'Once upon a time there was . . .'?
    Fairy stories or nursery tales.

b) Is this narrative also a nursery tale or children's story?
c) What is the effect of the substitution of **will** for **was**? (See also
   Vocabulary III question 5.)
   *The most obvious answer is that **will** suggests a world in the future
   rather than of the past. **Will** also suggests a world of coercion where
   people **will** do what they are told with little freedom of choice.*
d) List some words which depict the world **outside** the house as
   unpleasant.
   'mud' 'grimy' 'contaminated' 'stale' 'dust' 'disease'
e) What words are associated with the **inside** of the house?
   'interesting' 'congenial' . . .
f) Would you like to live in such a house? (Remember you would have
   everything you could possibly require.)
g) What is the tone of these sentences?
   'Out along the wires and beams their wishes will go back. Back, by
   return, will come the fulfilment of them.'
   (Note the 'balance' of: will go / will come; out / back)
h) What are three advantages of living in this new world?
   Good health, every wish fulfilled, no need to go shopping.

The questions here can lead to more extensive discussion of human
psychological 'needs' and the nature of individual freedom. If learners
know George Orwell's *1984* or Aldous Huxley's *Brave New World*
comparisons might be invoked. Frayn may be creating 'a very private life'
in which privacy is impossible because the individual's needs are already
known and determined. These questions might be best followed up after
learners have written 'predictions'.

3 *Lady Chatterley's Lover*: D. H. Lawrence

The following questions can be answered from close study of the text.
a) What in the description of Tevershall indicates that it is a predomi-
   nantly mining community?
   *The constant repetition of 'black' and the reference 'black with coal-
   dust'.*
b) How does Lawrence use language in the first sentence of the extract
   to suggest that the blackness of Tevershall is all-pervasive?
   *One answer might be that the forms of the word **black** occupy a range
   of different grammatical positions; e.g. past participle: '**blackened**
   brick'; adjective: '**black** slate roofs'; qualifier: '**black** with coal-dust';
   complement: 'the pavements wet and **black**'.*
c) What, in particular, contributes to the sense of ugliness and dismal-
   ness in Tevershall?

The following questions are for open discussion.

d) What do the words **Primitive, Wesleyan** and **Congregational** convey?
   *They are all different religious denominations/groups; different
   churches or chapels would be attended by different groups of people.*
   What is the purpose of the narrator, in using the word 'primitive' in
   lower case (primitive) and upper case (Primitive)?

e) 'All the people who live in Tevershall lack humanity.' Do you agree
   that the narrator suggests this?

f) What is the narrator saying about the way the school children sing?
   (Standard Five was a school age-group.)

g) What would be the atmosphere inside a school in Tevershall?
   Comment here on the mixing of a chapel and a prison.

h) What kind of films, do you think, will be shown at the cinema in
   Tevershall?

7 Re-writing:
Literary and non-literary discourse

Part A   Notes

Aims

This unit is designed to enable learners to explore the nature of literary
language. It does this by providing opportunities for comparing the
language of literary and non-literary discourse, where possible on the
same theme.

The Approach

Re-writing fosters sensitivity to different styles of English and helps
learners to become aware of the range of purposes to which language is
put. The exercise can also give practice in writing in different registers. In
a manner close to that suggested for creative writing in Unit 5, the
response to language is developed 'from the inside'. By re-writing from
one discourse to another learners also come to appreciate some of the
conventions and constraints which govern language use.

  This unit is more 'open ended' than previous units. This is because of
the nature of the topic: an analysis of some of the features of literary
discourse. Not all of these are purely linguistic, of course, but our focus is
on the language in keeping with the integrated approach throughout the
book and because we believe that analysis of how language works in
different types of discourse can take us a long way towards a basic understanding of the nature of literature. There are no particular teaching
techniques suggested. Much of the work can be followed by learners
working on their own or in pairs, but the teacher can extend the work
suggested by introducing examples of language in different written contexts and by encouraging learners to find their own examples for further
study.

  It should be noted that we do not believe that there is a strict dividing
line between literary and non-literary text. Instead we prefer the notion
of a 'cline' or scale of literariness which simply states that some texts have
greater degrees of literariness than others. We have tried to select texts for

comparison which have similar subject matter but whose positions on this scale differ considerably, and we suggest this as an area for further work. It can be instructive to compare texts at opposite ends of the scale (see our example of a poem compared with telephone user instructions) and at points where differentiation is not always clear and straightforward (see the examples of literary descriptions compared with advertising language). There are no commentaries on particular texts in this unit; instead a number of discussion points are listed.

Techniques

The exercises in the unit are graded in an approximate order of difficulty. The general sequence is:

1 questions about thematically related texts moving from lower to higher order questions;
2 exercises which involve changing and substituting single words and phrases – an exercise similar to standard cloze procedure (which is also a main activity in Unit 8);
3 re-writing sentences;
4 completing whole texts in a defined style;
5 re-writing from non-literary to literary discourse.

The last exercise is difficult but learners should be encouraged to progress towards it. However, teachers will assess for themselves how quickly they can move along this continuum and how far assistance, perhaps in the form of particular models, needs to be provided. Further related activities can also be found as follow-up exercises: for example, writing a newspaper report of an event described in a novel or producing a flow-diagram of the plot of a short story.

The aim is that activity involving manipulation of language should lead to exploration and investigation at a more discursive level. Learners should also discover directly from the re-writing exercises that all language can be exploited for literary ends and that there is no one literary language. Teachers might also point out examples of how many literary works, especially modernist texts, deliberately exploit other discourse styles. The most striking example is James Joyce's *Ulysses*.

Part B   Features of literary discourse

This section provides some general observations about the way language is used in literary texts. Learners should be encouraged to think about them carefully and discuss them.

The nature of literary discourse is not easy to define and we have only described some of the more obvious linguistic features. This unit is intended to be exploratory. We hope you and your students will take our points and ideas further and add to them.

Here, then, is a summary of some of the most basic issues and questions in the study of literary discourse.

1   It is rare for a literary text to be accompanied by pictures or diagrams. The words used do point outwards to the world and we do judge some texts according to how accurate and truthful a picture of life they paint. But literature is not dependent on any other medium.

2   Words in literary texts are characterised by the fact that they also point inwards and make relations or patterns with other words in the text.

3   Literary language will tend to be 'polysemic' rather than 'monosemic'. That is, the language will tend towards multiple rather than single meanings.

4   In literary texts there is often a high concentration of metaphoric effects. Literature informs us about things but information is not a primary function.

5   The reader of a literary text is not explicitly exhorted to do anything or perform specific actions but such texts can change the way we see the world or, at least, enable us to see things from a different perspective.

6   In a literary text different levels of language (syntax, phonology, vocabulary, graphology, cohesive and discoursal patterns) work together to express or symbolise the content. The linguistic structures and patterns which are created draw the attention of the reader to the style in which a text is written. There will always be some relation between style and content in the literary texts we value and enjoy.

7   There are conventions and forms for literary texts but in a literary text different effects can be produced by conforming to or deviating from the conventions.

8   There is no such thing as a literary language. That is, there are no words which are exclusively literary (with the exception of some poeticisms and archaisms) and could not be employed in other contexts.

9   Conversely, there are some discourse types which rely on special words and phrases and we recognise them accordingly.

10   However, there is no single point where literary texts stop and non-literary texts start. Different texts have different degrees of literariness and it may be better to see texts along a continuum or scale of literariness. A good example of texts which are not exclusively literary but which contain features of literariness would be advertising copy.

11 Refer learners back to Unit 1 'Summary' and the reasons why non-literary texts are generally easier to summarise than literary ones.

Finally, it should be noted that this unit is not divided into sections as strictly as other units. There are, however, a higher number of *Exploitation* sections. This reflects the fact that this unit is conceived as more in the nature of an 'open-ended' discussion where the aim is to encourage further learner 'exploitation'.

8 Under the microscope: Introduction to stylistic analysis

Part A Notes

Aims

The main aim of this unit is to draw together work on the style and language of texts studied in those previous units which have a more explicitly linguistic orientation: Unit 4 *Read it aloud*, Unit 5 *On the inside*, Unit 6 *Words and their impact*.

Techniques

The first part of this unit uses the technique of gap-filling. Again the aim is to involve the learner directly with the text. Learners should be referred to Unit 6 if they have not had previous experience of this procedure.

The second part of the unit concentrates on 'scrambled sentences'. Here it is important to understand how much flexibility there is in the techniques of 'scrambled' and 'elastic sentences' (Unit 5), and how much pleasure as well as increased language competence can be derived from combining sentences in these ways. Practice in these exercises should be given on literary and non-literary text.

The Approach

This unit is not quite so 'open-ended' as some previous units. The aim is to guide the learner through a text very carefully. In the case of Hardy's 'The Oxen' this is done in the form of an extended commentary on the poem. In this way learners can be introduced to literary and critical discourse of a type which they can expect to find in books of literary criticism. To this end, and to provide contrast with our own points, we have included in this unit three commentaries from other sources.

Although there are a number of activities and opportunities for group and pair work, the main strategy here should be one of learner self-access. The teacher's role is to advise and to prompt questions, as well as to supplement and extend points as necessary. Disagreements should be invited, as long as they are substantiated by close reference to the text.

Part B   Texts for intensive study

1   'Futility': Wilfred Owen

Note: The gap-filling exercise for this poem must be completed before
the intensive study. For the gap-filling the orientation (p. 109) and the
instruction 'think of the word which will best fit the surrounding words'
should be sufficient to attempt the process. But this will by no means
exhaust the poem. The intensive study should be done after an interval of
at least a week from the gap-filling.

This poem is not so readily accessible as many others in *The Web of
Words*. The reader does not immediately know what frame of reference
is being engaged (this phrase was used in the Notes to Unit 1 above). For
this reason, given either the first line, or the first stanza of the poem, it
would be almost impossible to predict what follows.

   'Access' to the poem should be through a series of fairly 'closed' questions, each point leading on to another question, for which there is an
explicable link. There is therefore a sort of 'question discourse' in
addition to the obvious poetic discourse.

The teacher should be prepared to insert more questions into the following sequence if this is necessary.
a)   What is the setting for the poem?
     France.
b)   What time of year is it?
     Winter.
c)   Would the sun be hot at that time of year?
     No.
d)   Why does the poet say 'even in France'?
     'Even' the terrible battlefield had some aspects of normality.
e)   What is the implication of 'until this morning'?
     The sun will no longer wake him.
f)   Why will the sun no longer wake him?
     The 'him' of line 1 is now dead.
g)   The sun touched him 'gently' at home. This contrasts with his death.
     What word of opposite meaning is suggested?
     Violently.
h)   Can anything rouse him now?
     No.
i)   So why 'Move him into the sun' (l. 1)?
     It suggests a more normal, ordered world.
j)   What other features of the 'normal' world does the poet mention?
     The fields unsown.
k)   Who is the poet addressing?

> *He is soliloquising. The 'Futility' of the title is expanded to a discussion of a violent but pointless death.*

It should now be possible to approach lines 8–14 with a short sequence of much more 'open' questions. For the following questions no answers are suggested, and the teacher should avoid any indication that a single answer is 'right' at the expense of all others.

l)   What is the connection between 'seeds' (l. 8) and the preceding stanza?

m)   Does it seem to you that the poet has forgotten the soldier, the 'him' of line 1? If so, why?

n)   In what way are these lines a commentary on war?

o)   Do you detect any particular mood in the poet in these lines?

As a final point discuss whether the answer to a summary question such as 'What is it all about?' adequately conveys the poet's meaning in lines 8–14.

2   'A narrow Fellow in the Grass': Emily Dickinson

The following 'intensive study' again assumes that learners will have already done the rearranging of stanzas and word/phrase study on pages 117–18. This further study comprises a commentary on the poem. It may be used in one of the following ways:

1   The teacher reads the commentary aloud, and invites answers from individual learners at the pauses. This may be preferable with a very small group.

2   The teacher pre-records the commentary, and learners attempt answers individually, either at home or in a language laboratory, in self-access mode.

3   As 2 above but the commentary is played on a classroom cassette player, and learners have an answer sheet. This resembles a test, but can involve everybody more fully.

Play through the recorded version of the poem at least once before beginning the commentary.

COMMENTARY

'A narrow Fellow in the Grass / Occasionally rides'. 'Rides' is not a word you would usually apply to a snake. The more usual word would be . . . ? (*pause*). So what extra dimension is added to the snake by saying he 'rides'? (*pause*). Most people hate snakes, and are afraid of them. But here the snake is described as 'a spotted shaft'. Do you detect anything evaluative in that phrase? That is, is it something you hate, or like, or is it neutral? (*pause*). The narrator then recalls having bent down to touch a snake, thinking it was something else. What did he – the narrator is a man – think it was? (*pause*). And why couldn't he get hold of it? (*pause*). So what does this tell us about snakes in general – are they more, or less dangerous than people think? (*pause*). Who then are 'Nature's People'? (*pause*). And in what way does the narrator feel differently about 'this Fellow', that is, the snake? (*pause*). 'This Fellow' is itself an evaluative phrase. What does it suggest to you? (*pause*).

Part C   Further exploitation

Discuss 'A narrow Fellow in the Grass' briefly in comparison with Lawrence's 'Snake' (Unit 3), but do not press for likenesses which do not exist. Remember that 'Snake' is a narrative which this poem is not; and that it has heavy moral overtones, which this poem does not.

Take three or four noun groups which refer to a snake.

Lawrence	*Dickinson*
'yellow-brown slackness soft-bellied'	'A narrow Fellow'
'a guest in quiet'	'A spotted shaft'

Ask the learners to comment on how each phrase best serves the needs of the poet.

With advanced learners ask them to make a brief commentary on another poem by Emily Dickinson, for example: 'There's been a Death, in the Opposite House' (Student's Book pp. 115–16 and *Appendix 8*) with five pauses built in where questions have to be answered. The writer must be able to answer his or her own questions!

9 'The Moving Finger writes': Background

Part A Notes

The Approach

This unit considers samples of literary text in relation to their 'background'. This 'background' can consist of information deliberately withheld by the writer, information about the writer which may have influenced his or her writing, or some political, religious or psychological insights into the protagonists or their setting.

If a writer is fervently in favour or violently opposed to a particular social, political or religious ideology, its influence is likely to be marked in his or her literary work. It is at that point that 'background' becomes a vital feature of the text. To read that text without some knowledge of its 'background' would be like reading a play with one of the principal characters omitted.

The non-native reader will not necessarily share the cultural assumptions made by the writer and this background knowledge must therefore be filled in before he or she can fully appreciate the writer's intentions.

Aims

The purpose of providing 'background' is to provide help at just those points where lack of it devalues the text. The aim here is to add to the general store of background information for students of literature, to develop a technique of decision-taking so that they can decide when to refer to reference books and when to read on, and, finally, to acquire skills in basic research, so that they have some idea of where to look when further information is necessary. The reward comes when students find that their background store of knowledge provides them with the key to an otherwise difficult or incomprehensible text.

Techniques

No method for the teaching of literature is implied in dealing with 'background'. If the 'background' is provided by lecture then these texts will be more conventionally teacher-centred, and less obviously learner-centred than other sections of the book, though an attempt is made to work towards a 'do-it-yourself' approach on the part of the learner, that is, deciding exactly what 'background' might be necessary and finding it from library sources. This of course supposes the availability of an adequate library (and is a strong case for developing such a facility with all possible resources, where it does not exist, but where English literature is taught). The unit begins with a non-literary text, with a series of questions and notes which draw attention to the information gap as it occurs in newspaper reporting, and indicates how journalism provides the necessary 'background', and at what points. This exercise should be worked through carefully. It is difficult to predict at exactly what point assistance is necessary, but this unit incorporates a number of possible examples, and suggests others where the learner/reader may make his or her own investigations.

The 'method' for acquiring this 'background' could incorporate numerous classroom and/or library procedures: gap-filling, group quizzes, group writing project, lecture, notes followed by question and answer activities etc. These and others are all available and all are potentially 'good', in that they are likely to complete the missing dimension. But the 'project' should not be at the expense of the literary text which is being studied. That is, the learner/reader should not become more involved in the 'background' than in the text; and this does imply careful control and direction on the part of the teacher, though problems will probably not arise if the teacher ensures that 'background work' is never allowed to go on for too long.

Part B Texts for intensive study

1 'After the Battle': A. P. Herbert

We suggest that the background study is completed before the further, intensive study. This will again encourage learners to look at the poem as a whole, and hopefully lessen the difficulty of discrete lexical items.

The following questions can be answered from close study of the text.
a) Who does 'they' in line 1 refer to?
   Senior commanders, 'behind the lines'.
b) Who does 'you' in line 5 refer to?
   The General who will come to congratulate the soldiers.
c) The poet never uses the pronoun 'I'. Who does he identify with?
   His fellow soldiers who survived the battle.
d) What does 'those spaces in the mess' (l. 13) refer to?
   The soldiers who were killed in the battle.

e) Who does 'friends' (l. 20) refer to?
   (*As for question (d) above.*)
f) In what sense is 'your heroes' (l. 6) ironic?
   The 'heroes', of whom the poet is one, do not want to be involved in the war, and do not want the public recognition on parade. They are heroes in the eyes of others.

These questions are for open discussion.

g) Do you get the feeling that this poem was written shortly after the battle – that is, that it has 'immediacy'? If so, which lines contribute to this feeling? Does the poem 'Futility' (Unit 8) have immediacy?
h) The language of this poem varies between near colloquial ('so they are satisfied . . . ', l. 1) and more markedly poetic ('those hollows in the heart', l. 14). Identify examples of each. What is the effect of this 'mix' of language?
i) If we omit the reference to 'capricious car' (l. 5), K.C.B. (l. 12) and 'chateau door' (l. 28) where in the world could the ideas of this poem apply, at the present time? Why do you think we have singled out the above three references for omission? What do they reveal of the background?

2   *One Day in the Life of Ivan Denisovich*: Alexander Solzhenitsyn

Learners should complete the background study before attempting the following exercises, which should be done at least one week later.
   One purpose of *The Web of Words* is to give learners 'multiple strategies' for dealing with literary texts. This is developed further in Part IV of this Teacher's Book under the heading 'Combining the approaches'.

The following questions exploit this text as a preparation for Part IV. They should be answered orally and unusual or imaginative answers should be actively encouraged.

a) Someone has escaped and the prisoners are being kept waiting in the intense cold – after working an 11-hour day. Predict what follows.
b) Make six statements for ranking, based solely on this text. Begin (i) The prisoners are on the edge of a revolt. (Elicit (ii)–(vi) orally and write them on a blackboard or OHP. Modify suggestions for greater appropriacy if necessary.)
c) Imagine you are making a film or video of this scene. What questions do you need to ask? For example:
   i)   How many people?
   ii) What clothes are they wearing?
   etc.

d) Re-write this scene as a short poem. Begin:
    The cold bit deep and still we had to wait . . .
e) Paragraph 4 (ll. 9–17) contains a number of taboo words. Why? Does their inclusion add to or detract from the literary quality of the text?

For further exploitation of this text see page 140 of the Student's Book.

Part C Further exploitation

Re-read 'After the Battle' in conjunction with 'The General' (Unit 4) and 'Futility' (Appendix 7). It is important that learners should prepare in advance of the exercise. Ask learners to develop sentences on the structures:

1 All three . . . but X is the most . . . of the three.
    e.g. *All three* deal with the horror of war, *but* 'Futility' *is the most* cerebral *of the three.*
2 The poems are all . . . but X is the only one with . . .
    e.g. *The poems are all* deeply personal, but 'The General' *is the only one with* a touch of humour to offset the bitterness.
3 X is . . . Y is . . . but Z is . . .
    e.g. 'Futility' *is* calm and detached; 'The General' *is* lively and spirited; but 'After the Battle' *is* bitter and angry.

Read aloud the following, which is from the opening of Chapter 3 of *The Prime of Miss Jean Brodie* (see Unit 4):

> The days passed and the wind blew from the Forth.
> It is not to be supposed that Miss Brodie was unique at this point of her prime; or that (since such things are relative) she was in any way off her head. She was alone, merely, in that she taught in a school like Marcia Blaine's. There were legions of her kind during the nineteen-thirties, women from the age of thirty and upward, who crowded their war-bereaved spinsterhood with voyages of discovery into new ideas and energetic practices in art or social welfare, education or religion. The progressive spinsters of Edinburgh did not teach in schools, especially in schools of traditional character like Marcia Blaine's School for Girls. It was in this that Miss Brodie was, as the rest of the staff spinsterhood put it, a trifle out of place. But she was not out of place amongst her own kind.
>
> *The Prime of Miss Jean Brodie*: Muriel Spark
> (Reproduced by kind permission of the author.)

Then ask the students if they think it is possible to enjoy *The Prime of Miss Jean Brodie* without this background information. Is this 'internalised background'?

In the light of the above extract ask them to discuss:
'Miss Brodie is perfectly normal. The school (Marcia Blaine's) was just not ready for her.'

10   In the forum:
Reading and discussing literature

Part A   Notes

Aims

The purpose of this unit is to give learners the opportunity to discuss
literature which will then give them confidence for further discussions.
Units 1–9 offer an introduction to language-based techniques and
approaches to description and interpretation of literature. This unit
provides learners with the chance to express their views and evaluate
texts. It comes at the end of the book because evaluation is meaningless
unless it is built on a sound descriptive and interpretive basis.

The Approach

Literature possesses a marked potential for discussion, and we have
chosen 'forum' as a convenient term for the exploitation of this potential.
Refined, formalised and transferred to the written form, this process
would be generally described as 'criticism'. If a learner is required to
produce a piece of criticism, it is likely to be an individual activity in
which he or she states both sides of an argument and evaluates the
author's aims. The audience will probably be the teacher. 'Forum' implies
interaction, in this case with peers.

The learners read a text and are given a lead. For the purposes of the
classroom, they are invited to argue for or against some aspect of the text,
or an author's view. In this activity the learners will not, of course, always
be expressing their own opinions, but will be role-playing.

For such activities there are no distinctions between prose and poetry.
Topic is more important than form. Reaction and response to the text is
what is required.

Techniques

Reacting to a text in this way is a fairly advanced level exercise, requiring
a thorough understanding of the text, with its implications and infer-
ences, and an ability to support and refute arguments.

The teacher may give help as he or she considers necessary in presenting the text initially, though in the case of longer texts reading should be done in advance of the class. Earlier 'approaches' may be used to 'penetrate' the texts, at the teacher's discretion.

For longer texts a further skill is required, and this is the ability to select key points in the text, which we refer to as 'pivotal points'. These represent actions or words on which the story hinges. Learners might find the following sentences useful when referring to these 'pivotal points' in their arguments:

'Do you remember when X (does something)?' or

'You're forgetting that Y (does something)' or

'I'm sure I'm right, because Z (does something).'

Summary (see Unit 1) is an aid to detecting the 'pivotal points' but further practice is included in this unit. Thereafter only extensive reading and discussion can develop the ability to seize quickly on such points, and use them to advantage, though the teacher might encourage more ranking exercises (see Unit 3) as a means to increasing confidence.

Learners should be divided into groups of three or four, with briefing as to the point they have to argue. They are then given time to prepare their discussion points. This time needs careful gauging. One spokesperson then presents the case for each group.

Obviously the degree to which the text provides material for the discussion varies considerably. *Forum I*, for example, provides very little. It is straightforward:

'Character A was right/wrong when he said . . . '

Forum III, however, provides a great deal of material and involves more considered argument, for example:

'Character B was good/bad, because he (did something).'

This point will probably be countered with a further 'pivotal point' from the other group.

Part B Texts for intensive study

1 *Othello*: Shakespeare

We are assuming that the class will attempt some of the recommended approaches in the Student's Book before beginning intensive study. All these approaches, including the 'forum' exercise, are designed to help the learner to focus on the issues involved in the argument. It is, of course, accepted that Shakespearean verse presents difficulties for learners. Nonnative speakers are all too often intimidated by the unfamiliar 'idiom'. It is, however, often quite possible for them to guess at the meaning by considering (a) the context and (b) those words in the phrase which they already know.

The following practice is intended to help learners to overcome this 'fear of the idiom'. They should attempt to use colloquial present-day English to explain the Shakespearean expression. Discourage the term 'paraphrase' as it will limit the learners' interpretation of the verse. Learners should then be able to apply the technique either to the play as a whole, or to other plays. We suggest you use the following as an example. (In spite of the seriousness of the play keep as a theme 'Enjoy your Shakespeare'.)

> I humbly do beseech you of your pardon (l. 69)
> pardon – forgiveness
> *Please forgive me.*

a) I perchance am vicious in my guess (l. 2)
   It is perhaps wicked of me to suggest it.
b) Robs me of that which not enriches him (l. 17)
   He steals something which is no good to him.
c) What damned minutes tells he o'er (l. 26)
   How he suffers!
d) Poor and content is rich, and rich enough (l. 29)
   You can be quite happy, even if you're poor, if your mind is at rest.
e) There is no more but this (l. 48)
   I have to decide between the following . . .
f) Wear your eye thus (l. 55)
   Don't show any special emotion.

Extend this list with a further five or six examples. Allow fairly 'free' interpretation. Ask learners to work in pairs and ask each other for a gloss of still further examples, consulting a third person, but not the teacher, for adjudication. Treat the whole as a 'fun' exercise.

Iago's speeches in this extract are a subtle form of 'winning Othello's mind'. Thus in lines 1–11 he says in effect:
   'Don't listen to me' – as a way of ensuring that Othello does listen to
   him.
Ask learners to make similar 'reports' on each of Iago's speeches. (The exercise combines summary and inference. Learners must themselves present the inference without being asked, directly, an inferential question, for example, 'Why does Iago say:
   "I entreat you . . . take no notice"' (ll. 5–7)?
This exercise is best done orally first, with written follow-up.

Further exploitation is recommended in the Student's Book on page 150.

Beyond that, study should extend to the play as a whole, and not be limited to the extract used here.

2 'The Force of Circumstance': W. Somerset Maugham

The Student's Book has only a limited range of tasks for this story. Of these tasks the 'Forum' exercise is (a) evaluative and (b) discursive. Other exercises ('pivotal points') are related to summary (Unit 1) and vocabulary (Unit 6). The Teacher's Book has indicated that question types can, and should, be varied, for any text, but should always aim to elicit something which is not immediately obvious to the learner. One further area, related to background (Unit 9), is an investigation of what may be called 'cross-cultural' features. The longer text allows an opportunity to examine some of these, which may cause difficulties for the reader from a different cultural background. For example, take a sentence such as: 'He walked down the street eating his fish and chips'. Consider the implications for a British reader. Are these immediately evident to an Indian, Japanese or Brazilian reader? The following questions are not intended to exhaust cross-cultural points, but are intended again as a sensitising process for the student of literature. The latter must be able to decide how important or unimportant each of these is, and whether further investigation is necessary.

For the following questions there are no 'correct' answers. Omit any questions where the answer would be 'completely obvious' for your learners. (Page numbers refer to the Student's Book.)
a) 'She had met him at a small place by the seaside where she was spending a month's holiday with her mother.' (p. 153, ll. 60–1)
   What does this tell us about Doris's social level?
b) 'He asked her to marry him at the end of the month's holiday. She had known he was going to, and had decided to refuse him.' (p. 153, ll. 70–1)
   What are the conventions here regarding proposals of marriage?
c) '... the bath-houses were under the bedrooms, on the ground; you had a large tub of water and you sluiced yourself with a little tin pail.' (p. 154, ll. 100–2)
   What can we infer about the climate?
   What can we infer about the general amenity of the place where Guy and Doris were living?
d) ' "The old Sultan didn't think it was a white woman's country," he said presently. "He rather encouraged people to – keep house with native girls." ' (p. 156, ll. 171–3)
   What does this indicate about racial attitudes, in particular:
   i) the Sultan's attitude towards European women?

ii)   the attitude of European men towards the women of the country?

e)   'She felt an inordinate pride because it was her house (she had never in her life lived in anything but a poky flat) and she had made it charming for him.' (p. 157, ll. 245–8)
What is implied by a 'poky flat'?
How do you interpret 'charming' when applied to the main room of a house?

f)   'The tennis-court was two or three hundred yards from the bungalow and after tea . . . ' (p. 158, ll. 276–7)
What pattern of social behaviour is implied by the words 'after tea'?

Ask learners to find a further three points in the story where there is a possibility of 'cross-cultural difficulty'.

Extend this to any further story and/or novel. Learners should bring to the lesson an example which they find genuinely puzzling. There should be a context, and the example should be at least of sentence length.

Part C   Further exploitation

For further exploitation examine carefully the language attributed to Doris. This is very 'marked', indicating: (a) middle- or upper-class informality and (b) period (i.e. phrases which may have been common in the 1920s, but would sound dated today). For example:

i)   'Isn't that baby a duck?' (p. 158, l. 294)
ii)   'What is it, old man? Tell mother.' (p. 159, l. 343)

Ask learners to find as many examples of this as they can. This is an advanced exercise, and can be combined with socio-linguistic studies if the learners also study linguistics. If learners have no formal knowledge of linguistics explain it simply in terms of 'examining the dialogue'.

Discuss informally if the ending to the story was accurately predicted or not. Cross reference to Unit 1 Prediction.

DESCRIPTION, INTERPRETATION AND EVALUATION:
A FINAL NOTE

The relationship between these categories is a complex one. The most difficult task for native and non-native readers of literature (particularly non-native) is evaluation. Learners sometimes say that they do not like a text, or prefer one to another, but this can have as much to do with level of difficulty as with evaluation of the inter-relations between the language or expression, and their own experience of the nature of the messages a work conveys. But it is important for learners to express opinions, and their likes and dislikes, as well as to make discriminations between texts. It is, of course, difficult to divorce analysis and experience of language from analysis of experience readers have lived and shared themselves, as individuals. In reading a literature in a foreign language there is, even more than with the native speaker, an inevitable shuttling back and forth between analysing the experiences conveyed and analysing the language which mediates them. In this unit more opportunities than in previous units are provided for expressions of viewpoint and for evaluation, but it comes at the end of the book because we believe there is little point to evaluation unless it is built on sound descriptive and interpretative skills. In the development of these skills the ability to analyse language, though in many ways preliminary and pre-literary, is crucial. This book has tried to supply language-based techniques and approaches to description and interpretation.

We do not pretend to have supplied more than starting points but we hope that you and your students have found that these language-based bricks will contribute to laying the foundations of an integrated development of some important aspects of both language and literary competence.

Section IV Combining the 'approaches'

Each of the ten units in this book concentrates on a single 'approach'. Texts are 'recycled' in subsequent units; we hope this will encourage learners to study them using two or three different 'approaches'. Our aim in this section is to explore further the possibilities of combining 'approaches'.

We have selected three texts: *Cat in the Rain* by Hemingway, 'Futility' by Owen and 'Ozymandias' by Shelley. These texts are referred to repeatedly in the Student's Book. A series of steps for each text follows. We have selected a number of language-based 'approaches' for each one.

I 'Cat in the Rain'

1 Prediction

There are several places where prediction can be invited. For example:
a) Learners can be asked to invent an alternative title.
b) The wife is returning to her room and sees the hotel-keeper again (Unit 1 p. 7, ll. 62–3).
c) Learners can be asked to imagine what happens after the end of the story. They can be invited to supply a short paragraph in which they write an 'ending' to the story.

(c) is designed to draw attention to the structure of the story. Hemingway withholds a traditional ending which might contain a moral, judgement or resolution of the action. Again prediction of endings must be related to the learners' interpretation of the story so far.

2 Summary

We suggest the following procedure:
a) Learners write a summary or summaries (of different lengths) according to instructions.
b) Summaries are compared. Learners should see that (i) no summary is, of course, adequate, (ii) any selection of what happens in the story

involved interpretation, (iii) merely to concentrate on 'what happens' does not capture the meanings between the lines of the text; but it probably does capture the narrative structure of a story in which the events themselves appear inconsequential and leave us with a feeling of 'so what'!

c) The point here is to help learners to begin to seek something more in their reading. Learners should be asked to justify what they have left out. The 25–30 word summary is particularly testing in this respect. How many learners left out reference to the rain or Italy or the hotel-keeper or the husband? Is it essential to say the couple were American?

3   Scrambled sentences and stylistic analysis

The steps within this sub-section are more numerous. Learners may need to be given practice first in combining sentences. For example:

a) How can these two sentences be combined into one?
   i)   I arrived at the station.
   ii) The station was crowded.
   Or, if (iii), (iv) and (v) are added, how can they be combined into one?
   iii) I waited for the train.
   iv) The train was an express.
   v)   The train was late.
   The point of this is (a) to give some language practice, (b) to prepare learners for working with the adapted 'literary' sentences below and (c) to begin to sensitise learners to the stylistic effects of repetition of words (where pronouns could be used) and of simple main clause sentence structures.

b) Now take some sentences which resemble closely those written by Hemingway:
   i)   The Americans stayed at the hotel.
   ii) The hotel faced the sea.
   iii) The hotel was in the square.
   iv) The war-monument was in the square.
   v)   The war-monument was made of bronze.
   Re-write them as one sentence. If this is too difficult begin by combining (i–iii) and then (iv–v) separately.

c) Here is what Hemingway wrote in the first paragraph of 'Cat in the Rain':

> There were only two Americans stopping at the hotel. They did not know any of the people they passed on the stairs on their way to and from their room. Their room was on the second floor facing the sea. It also faced the public garden and the war monument. There were big

palms and green benches in the public garden. In the good weather there was always an artist with his easel. Artists liked the way the palms grew and the bright colours of the hotels facing the gardens and the sea. Italians came from a long way off to look up at the war monument. It was made of bronze and glistened in the rain. It was raining. The rain dripped from the palm trees. Water stood in pools on the gravel paths. The sea broke in a long line in the rain and slipped back down the beach to come up and break again in a long line in the rain. The motor-cars were gone from the square by the war monument. Across the square in the doorway of the café a waiter stood looking out at the empty square.

Ask learners to consider the following questions.
1 Why are so many of the sentences written in the same clause pattern? That is, main clause, followed by main clause with no subordinate clauses.
2 Why are so many nouns repeated? It would be more useful for pronouns to replace the repeated noun. Clause patterns are repeated. Nouns are repeated. Why?
3 One sentence, in particular, contains a repetition which means that at the end it comes back to the point at which it began. Which sentence is it? Why is it written in this way?

d) Another exercise also related to the first paragraph of 'Cat in the Rain' is to count the number of adjectives. How many can they find? Why does Hemingway use so few adjectives (and adverbs)?
To help learners clarify these thoughts, ask them to write an 'elastic sentence' – that is, one which can be made to stretch. Ask them to take any one sentence from that first paragraph and re-write it adding as many adjectives as possible.
Here is an example of what can be done with the final sentence:
Across the deserted gloomy square in the poorly-lit doorway of the Italian-style café a well-dressed young waiter stood looking out at the unfamiliar, desolate and empty square.
Ask learners what is different about this sentence and the sentences they have written. It should be a little easier now to answer the question: 'Why has Hemingway used this kind of style?' To summarise:
1 The style is repetitive in clause pattern and in lexical pattern. There is little variety.
2 The cohesion or joining up of sentences is not varied in any way.
3 The absence of adjectives makes the scene bare and colourless and empty.

e) Is there a link between language form and literary meaning? That is, between the atmosphere of the scene and the monotonous repetition, lack of variety and emptiness.

A key sentence here may be:

'The American wife stood at the window, looking out.'

It is the American wife's view. It is the scene that she sees. A summary would probably not have mentioned her feelings. Hemingway does not mention her feelings directly, either. But the style can convey those feelings to us indirectly. Hemingway does not write in the text that she is bored or that her life is monotonous and repetitive. But the lack of variety in the linguistic patterning of the style together with the drab, empty and lifeless scene does encourage the reader to make this kind of link. The sentence:

'The sea broke in a long line in the rain and slipped back down the beach to come up and break again in a long line in the rain.'

comes back to the point at which it began. It is circular and repetitive. In her search for the cat the American wife leaves her room but comes back again to where she started from. Although it is difficult to summarise this opening paragraph, it is important for our understanding of the story. How it is written (i.e. its style) is an important part of what is being said.

4 Gap-filling

This is an 'approach' which does not combine easily with others. It is always best done as a first 'approach' because once the text has been read then readers may easily recall the omitted items. However, it may be tackled at this stage in a limited fashion. Two words, one lexical, the other grammatical, could be blanked out:

a) 'empty' from the end of the first paragraph
b) 'a' from the penultimate paragraph when the maid brings the cat up to the American couple's room.

In (a) the word 'empty' describes the square but may also convey something of the feeling of emptiness of the American wife who is looking out into the square. Learners might be given a choice here from: 'deserted', 'quiet', 'wet', 'empty'.

In (b) there are at least two possibilities. Learners can be asked to complete the sentence: 'She held . . .' (where the emphasis is more on predicting narrative outcomes). If the focus is more stylistic, given the sentence 'She held .... big tortoiseshell cat pressed tight against her' they can be asked whether 'the' or 'a' should be inserted in the gap. The choice here is closely connected with an interpretation of whether or not the cat is the same one the wife was looking for:

She held a big tortoiseshell cat (different cat).

She held the big tortoiseshell cat (same cat).

This then leads to discussion of the word 'big' (which could also be omitted) and its relationship to 'kitty'.

5   Scenario

There is a lot of scope here for inviting a class to say how they would 'film' this story. How would the husband's role be played and how would his immobility be best filmed? How would the opening paragraph be best represented on film?

How would the couple talk to each other? How would the class read aloud the exclamations of the American wife towards the end of the story (see Unit 1 p. 8, ll. 90–100)? Again, how would that opening paragraph be best read aloud? What are the relevant variables?

6   Forum

This is generally best left to the end of the work on the story. It is designed to encourage discussion and to allow learners to draw on their own experience where possible. In Unit 10 the following opposing propositions are suggested for debate:

A   George is level-headed and contented. His wife cannot settle and is neurotic. She behaves like a little child and George has to be firm with her. The rift in the relationship is the wife's fault.

B   George is selfish and insensitive to his wife's needs. She wants more care and attention. The rift in the relationship is George's fault.

In case learners feel that B is the more obviously 'correct' interpretation refer them to (a) the wife's use of the word 'kitty' – a word used of cats by children (b) the fact that she is also referred to in the story as the American 'girl' (c) the way she uses the phrase 'I want . . . I want . . . I want . . .' (see Unit 1 p. 8, ll. 90–100).
Hopefully, learners will come to recognise the essential indeterminacy of this story. There is no single correct interpretation.

II   'Futility'

1   Gap-filling

The purpose of this sub-section is to suggest that 'approaches' can be usefully combined in order to exploit this text. In Unit 8 the poem was explored by means of gap-filling exercises. This is clearly the approach to this text which is best completed first. Further work can be undertaken with reference to Unit 6 pages 88–90.

2   Re-writing

The technique here is a little different from Unit 7 where different registers
are used and where prose texts are a focus. Here the re-writing is from
poetry into prose. The re-writing should draw attention to the reasons for
the ordering of clauses or sentences. For example, learners can be asked
to compare lines from the poem with re-written versions:

a)   Gently its touch awoke him once,
     At home, whispering of fields unsown.

> *Re-write:* Its rays once gently awoke him,
>   At home, the whispering of the unsown fields.

What is the effect of 'gently' at the beginning of the line?
What is the effect of the reversal of adjective and noun in 'fields
unsown'?

b)   Always it woke him, even in France,
     Until this morning and this snow.

> *Re-write:* Until this morning and this snow
>   It always woke him, even in France.

What is the effect of the placement of 'always' at the beginning of the
sentence/line?
What happens to the rhythm of reading (rising/falling intonation)
when the adverbial phrase 'Until this morning and this snow' comes
in the first line? What was Owen's purpose in putting it in second
position? (One view might be that the falling rhythm of 'Until this
morning and this snow' conveys a cold sadness and finality which
contrasts with the optimism of 'always' – reinforced by the stress it
receives from its line-initial position.)

c)   Are limbs, so dear-achieved, are sides,
     Full-nerved – still warm – too hard to stir?

> *Re-write:* Are warm, dear-achieved limbs and
>   warm full-nerved sides too hard to stir?

What is the effect of reading these two questions aloud? One is much
more broken, staccato and uneven than the other. Which one? Why?
What is Owen's purpose in selecting this style for the theme or topic
he is conveying?

3   Background

War poems such as this provide excellent starting points for thematic
comparison. Compare, for example, the different treatments of war in

'After the Battle' and 'The General' (Unit 4). 'Futility' can also be extended with reference to its background. The passage describing the war (Unit 9 p. 137) can be used and learners asked to make up 4–5 questions about this poem: answers should be obtainable by reference to the passage.

III 'Ozymandias'

1 Ranking

In Unit 3 this poem formed the basis of a true/false exercise (p. 42). Equally, a series of statements, focussed on the character of Ozymandias, could be made up for ranking. One main point, which should emerge from this exercise, is that Shelley does not reveal much explicitly about Ozymandias' character. Learners have to read between the lines and disagreements can occur. The true/false exercise highlights this. The column marked (?) might thus attract a tick (√) but so might another column. For example:

	T	*F*	(?)
Ozymandias was a king who killed lots of people	√		√

Close reference to the text cannot 'prove' this is true but learners might be encouraged to argue from lines 4–5 and 10–11 that he is unlikely to have had such ambitions without killing those who got in his way. The point is that the exercise should demonstrate the need for a (?) column in a literary text. Literary texts do not deal with *true* and *false* in such exclusive terms.

2 Scrambled sentences and stylistic analysis

The last three lines of the poem may be of especial significance in this respect. The following re-writing of the relevant sentences can aid appreciation of Shelley's stylistic effects:
The sands are lonely and flat.
The sands are vast and bare.
The sands stretch far away.

Learners can be invited to combine these sentences into one. For example:
The lonely and flat sands, which are vast and bare, stretch far away.

Comparison with Shelley's version can draw attention to the alliterative use of the words 'lone' and 'level' and 'boundless' and 'bare' in the original text, to the link in sound between 'away' and 'decay' and to the consequent emphasis on 'stretch far away' as the final element in the poem. The long sentence here also contrasts with and highlights the short sentence 'Nothing beside remains' which takes on another emphasis, especially after the quoted statement of Ozymandias.

3 Reading aloud

Work on 1 and 2 above should raise questions of interpretation. Such questions will affect how the poem is read aloud. Particular decisions will be needed on the following: lines 4–5 smiling – grim? lines 10–12 loud – soft / quick – slow? How will 'Nothing beside remains' be read? Will it contrast with Ozymandias' words? Will a pause between lines help the contrast? And should the final lines be read in the same way?

4 Scenario

There is considerable scope here; and the translation from verbal analysis to visual representation can assist greater appreciation of Shelley's use of language. Questions of interpretation which need resolving would include:

line 1	How is the remoteness of the monument from the 'I' conveyed? How far has the traveller had to travel?
line 2	How is the sense of size represented on film ('vast', 'colossal')? Close up? Camera moves slowly away, panning up?
line 5	Close up? Flash-back using 'live' actor?
line 9	Inset.
lines 10–11	Soundtrack.
line 12	Duration of filming surrounding sands? Continue voice-over?
lines 13–14	As for line 12 above. Link with presentation of line 1?

The suggestions for combining approaches above are only outlines of a method. They are not the only way it can be done. Singly and collectively they are stages on the way to a fuller engagement with and interpretation of the text.

Section V   Biographical notes

Kingsley Amis (born 1922) is a novelist, journalist and poet. His first novel *Lucky Jim* (1954, Somerset Maugham Award) brought him popular success. He is best known for his comic satires but has shown his versatility in writing many different types of novel. In 1986 he won the Booker Prize for his novel *The Old Devils*. He has also published several collections of poems.

George Barlow (1847–1913) is a minor novelist and poet associated most clearly with the late Victorian period. He wrote the libretto in English of Gounod's *Ave Maria* at the composer's request. He also wrote an epic *The Pageant of Life* (1888).

Robert Browning (1812–89) is best known for his mastery of the dramatic monologue in poetry but he never achieved the success of Tennyson during his own lifetime. His volumes *Men and Women* (1855) and *Dramatis Personae* (1864) continue, however, to attract considerable critical attention. He was married to Elizabeth Barrett.

Barry Cole (born 1936) is a novelist and poet. His first volume of poetry *Moonsearch* was published in 1968. A further volume *The Rehousing of Scaffardi* was published in 1976. From 1970–2 he was a fellow in literature at the universities of Durham and Newcastle.

Joseph Conrad (1857–1924) is one of the greatest novelists in the English language, although he was born Jozef Teodor Konrad Nalecz Korzeniowski in the Polish Ukraine and did not begin to learn English until he worked as a merchant seaman. Most of his novels and stories reflect his naval experience. His best known novels are *Lord Jim* (1900); *Nostromo* (1904); *The Secret Agent* (1907) and *Under Western Eyes* (1911).

Charles Dickens (1812–70) is the English writer who comes closest to Shakespeare in the extent and durability of his reputation and in his adoption as a national English literary figure. Dickens' novels have become especially popular in recent times due to cinema and television adaptations. Dickens' greatest novels include: *David Copperfield* (1849); *Little Dorrit* (1855); *Great Expectations* (1860) and *Our Mutual Friend* (1864).

Emily Dickinson (1830–86) was a recluse for most of her life staying in the small New England Puritan town of Amherst. She wrote a remarkably large number of poems (over 1700) although only two were published in her own lifetime. Her poems are often indirect or allegorical revealing little overtly of her own feelings or personality. She is probably the best known American woman poet.

George Eliot (1819–80) was a woman writer. Her real name was Mary Ann Evans and the name George Eliot was adopted as a pen-name. George Eliot was very much at the centre of the intellectual and literary life of her day but only started writing novels after a long period as a translator and reviewer. Her novel *Middlemarch* (1871) is one of the most important novels in the English language. Other novels include: *The Mill on the Floss* (1860) and *Daniel Deronda* (1874).

Michael Frayn (born 1933) is a journalist, humorous columnist, novelist and playwright. Several of his recent plays, which include *Clouds*, *Alphabetical Order*, *Noises Off* have enjoyed long periods of success on the London stage. He has also translated modern Russian poetry and drama into English and written a number of humorous novels including *The Russian Interpreter* (1966). *A Very Private Life* was first published in 1968.

Oliver Goldsmith (1730–74) was a journalist, essayist, dramatist and novelist. His play *She Stoops to Conquer* (1773) has been immensely successful and is still regularly performed today. His most successful long poem is *The Deserted Village* (1770), which captures the spirit of migration from the countryside to the rapidly growing industrial towns in the latter half of the eighteenth century.

Thomas Hardy (1840–1928) was born in the West Country of England (referred to in his fiction as Wessex) and wrote mostly with this region as the setting for his work. He is best known and most widely studied as a novelist but his poetry has had an extensive influence on many twentieth century poets. Much of his work is concerned with the clash between Victorian ideas and values and the anxiety of modern living. His most famous novels are *Tess of the D'Urbervilles* (1891); *Far From the Madding Crowd* (1874) and *Jude the Obscure* (1895). The last thirty years of his life were devoted exclusively to poetry and to verse drama.

Ernest Hemingway (1899–1961) is a master of the art of the short story and a major figure in modern American literature. Hemingway was one of several American writers who were based in Paris in the 1920s and many of his stories and novels have an international character and deal with action such as big-game hunting in Africa and bull-fighting in Spain. His best known works include *For Whom the Bell Tolls* (1940) and *The Old Man and the Sea* (1952).

W. E. Henley (1849–1903) is a minor Victorian poet who was also an editor and critic. His collection *The Song of the Sword* was published in 1892.

A. P. Herbert (1890–1971) is known as a humourist, journalist, novelist and poet. His novel *The Secret Battle* (1919) catalogues his experiences of the First World War. He also wrote legal satires, for example, *Misleading Cases in Common Law* (1929) and was an M.P. 1935–50.

George Herbert (1593–1633) is best known for his religious poetry. His output was not extensive and *The Temple* (1633) is his only collection of poems. He is regularly grouped with poets such as Donne and Vaughan in the school of 'metaphysical poets'.

A. E. Housman (1859–1936) wrote verse of sustained pessimism and bleakness typified by *A Shropshire Lad* (1896). As well as writing poetry, Housman was a Latin scholar and was appointed Professor of Latin at the University of Cambridge in 1911. His lecture *The Name and Nature of Poetry* was published in 1933.

Charles Kingsley (1819–75) is known primarily for his novels, which are often set in the past of Elizabethan England or Viking Britain and which evoke Christian socialist values; best known, however, is his children's fantasy, *The Water Babies* (1863).

D. H. Lawrence (1885–1930) is one of the greatest and most controversial of modern novelists. Like Virginia Woolf, he experimented with the form of the novel but also treated themes such as the sexual relations between men and women with greater explicitness than hitherto. Lawrence spent many years travelling restlessly throughout the world in search of a more humane society. His most widely read novels include the semi-autobiographical *Sons and Lovers* (1913), *The Rainbow* (1915), *Women in Love* (1920), and the particularly controversial *Lady Chatterley's Lover* (1928) which remained censored until 1961.

W. Somerset Maugham (1874–1965) was a prolific writer of short stories, plays and novels (his *Collected Works* 1934–50 are in twenty volumes) who travelled extensively and who set many of his writings in South America and the Far East. He is recognised as a master of the short story genre though his novels have been less well received. Major novels are: *Of Human Bondage* (1915), *The Moon and Sixpence* (1919) and *The Razor's Edge* (1944).

Edwin Morgan (born 1920) is one of Britain's foremost 'concrete' poets. Until 1980, he was Professor of English Literature at the University of Glasgow. He has also translated Italian, Spanish and Russian poetry into English (poets such as Montale, Balli, Neruda and Mayakovsky). His *Poems of Thirty Years* was published in 1982.

Wilfred Owen (1893–1918) is the best known of the First World War poets and probably its most technically inventive. Although influenced in his early poetry by John Keats, his poetry is unromantic and unheroic. He has had a lasting influence on the tone and style of much modern poetry.

Harold Pinter (born 1930) is one of Britain's most highly regarded living playwrights. He first worked as an actor but his first play *The Room* was published in 1957. His plays frequently explore the 'psychological space' between characters and can be by turns comic, menacing and disturbing. There is rarely much overt 'action' in the plays. His plays include *The Caretaker* (1960), *The Homecoming* (1964) and *Betrayal* (1978).

Craig Raine (born 1944) is one of Britain's most highly acclaimed poets. He is the founder of what is sometimes jokingly referred to as 'the Martian school' of poetry which is based on the presentation of an out-sider's view of contemporary society by a series of witty metaphoric analogies. He is currently Poetry Editor of the English publishing house Faber and Faber in London.

Christina Rossetti (1830–94) is a minor Victorian poet best known for her religious poetry. Her main volume *The Prince's Progress* was published in 1866.

Siegfried Sassoon (1886–1967) is, like Wilfred Owen, associated primarily with the poetry of the First World War, although his poetry is more sharply satiric than that of Owen. His verse output was limited but he also wrote prose works such as the popular *Memoirs of a Fox-Hunting Man* (1928).

Vernon Scannell (born 1922) is a poet best known for his treatment of domestic subjects and common human interests in informal colloquial language. His *New and Collected Poems 1950–80* appeared in 1980 and he has also written several novels and an autobiography *The Tiger and The Rose* (1971).

William Shakespeare (1564–1616) is the 'national poet' of England and the greatest figure in the history of English language and literature. His thirty-seven plays exhibit a remarkable technical, generic and thematic range and together with his one hundred and fifty-four sonnets are among the most widely studied and analysed of texts in English. His plays are regularly performed, most prominently in Stratford-upon-Avon (his birthplace) and in London.

Percy Bysshe Shelley (1792–1822) is one of the great English Romantic poets and the one who was most committed to ideas of freedom and revolution leading to a more humane and democratic society. He travelled widely in Europe and was drowned at an early age off the coast near Livorno, Italy. He wrote many short lyrics but is probably best known for his longer poems such as *Prometheus Unbound* (1820) and *Adonais* (1821) which was an elegy to the death of Keats.

Alexander Solzhenitsyn (born 1918) is a Soviet Russian writer whose works have been translated into many languages. His novels *Cancer Ward*, *The First Circle* and *August 1914* are major works in the tradition of Tolstoy and Dostoevsky. However, he has been criticised in the Soviet Union for taking an anti-Soviet stance and in 1974 he was arrested and deported to the West. In 1970 he won the Nobel Prize for Literature.

Muriel Spark (born 1918) is best known for a range of witty and some-times savagely comic stories and novels. Her most popular success is *The Prime of Miss Jean Brodie* (1961) which was also a successful film, play and television series. Other well-received novels are *The Driver's Seat* (1970), *Memento Mori* (1959), *The Mandelbaum Gate* (1965).

Edmund Spenser (1552–99) is one of the major English poets of the Elizabethan era. He is a master of the sonnet form and in his longer poems developed new stanzaic forms. He wrote *The Shepheardes Calender* (1579) and his major work *The Fairie Queen* (1590) was dedicated to Queen Elizabeth I. His poetry considerably influenced Milton and Keats.

Alfred Lord Tennyson (1809–92) is the poet most completely associated with the Victorian Age and was a poet laureate. His reputation has declined in this century although his work is being currently re-evaluated, particularly for Tennyson's ability to represent and explore the contradictions of his age. His best known long poems are *In Memoriam* (1850) and *Idylls of the King* (1859).

D. M. Thomas (born 1935) was a teacher and lecturer in English Literature but now writes novels and poetry full-time. His novels *Birthstone* (1980) and *Ararat* (1983) were well-received but his novel *The White Hotel* (1981) was published to critical acclaim and won numerous literary awards. He has also published five volumes of poetry.

John Updike (born 1932) is an American novelist, short story writer and poet. After graduating, he worked on *The New Yorker* as a reporter for two years and his first work was published in that magazine. He soon gained a reputation as an observer of modern American life. *The Centaur* (1963, National Book Award) is considered by many to be his best work.

H. G. Wells (1866–1946) was a prolific writer of essays, short stories and novels. He is probably best known popularly for his science fiction (e.g. *The Time Machine*, 1895; *The War of the Worlds*, 1898). But his critical reputation as a traditional novelist has grown steadily since his death. Among his most widely read novels are *Tono-Bungay* (1909), *The History of Mr. Polly* (1910) and *Kipps* (1905).

Walt Whitman (1819–92) is one of the greatest American poets and his best known volume *Leaves of Grass* (1855) has been extremely influential on modern poetry. Whitman was an essentially lyric poet who devoted much of his poetry to a celebration of nineteenth century democratic ideals.

Virginia Woolf (1882–1941) is a major novelist best known for her 'modernist' experimentation with the form of the novel and, specifically, for the development of techniques which reflect the inner workings of the human mind. Her main novels are *Mrs Dalloway* (1925), *To the Lighthouse* (1927), and *The Waves* (1931). Virginia Woolf was a feminist very much concerned with the rights of women and with the promotion of writing by women. She committed suicide during one of several mental breakdowns.

W. B. Yeats (1865–1939) was an Irishman whose work was always closely connected with the political and cultural crises of Ireland in this century. Yeats produced essays on a wide range of philosophical and aesthetic issues and also wrote plays but his main output was a body of poetry which puts him in the front rank of English poets. His poetry extends over sixty years with some of his best known poetry in *The Tower* (1928).